# Tree roots and buildings

# Tree roots and buildings
## *Second edition*

D F Cutler
I B K Richardson

Longman Scientific & Technical

**Longman Scientific & Technical,**
Longman Group UK Limited,
Longman House, Burnt Mill, Harlow,
Essex CM20 2JE, England
*and Associated Companies throughout the world.*

First published 1989
Second edition 1989
Second impression 1991

British Library Cataloguing in Publication Data
Cutler, D F (David Frederick)
   Tree roots and buildings. – 2nd ed.
   1. Buildings. Damage by roots of trees
   I. Title   II. Richardson, I B K
   693.8′5

ISBN 0-582-03410-8

Set in Linotron 202 11/12pt Baskerville
Produced by Longman Singapore Publishers (Pte) Ltd.
Printed in Singapore

*Dedicated to the memory of George Ernest Brown 1917–1980, former Assistant Curator at Kew, who gave much help and encouragement in this work.*

# Contents

# Preface to first edition

The value of trees in urban environments is now generally recognised. Their presence is important not only aesthetically but also socially in helping to make cities and towns agreeable places in which to live and work. It is, however, also well known that under certain conditions serious damage can be caused to buildings by neighbouring trees. The potential conflict of interests is obvious. It is my hope that the information in this book will help to resolve this.

The Jodrell Laboratory at the Royal Botanic Gardens, Kew, has long been an internationally renowned centre for research into comparative plant anatomy. For some years the Laboratory ran a service for identifying tree roots by their anatomical structure. So numerous were the enquiries that it was decided to expand the service in order to make a planned investigation into tree roots in relation to such factors as soil, damage to buildings, and also the growth of the tree itself. Thus was started the Kew Tree Root Survey under the supervision of Dr D F Cutler of the Jodrell Laboratory and with the collaboration of the arboriculturists at Kew. Careful thought was given to the sort of information to be collected, and this was organised on a standardised pattern.

In 1976 a Seminar was held at Kew on *Tree Roots and Damage to Buildings*. Some 220 people attended, representing a wide range of interests. As a result it became clear that the then existing knowledge was inadequate and often empirical and that there was an urgent need to make available authoritative guidance on tree planting in relation to buildings, based on quantifiable data.

It was therefore decided to accelerate the Survey and in 1977 Mr I B K Richardson was appointed on a two-year contract by the Bentham-Moxon Trust to assist with collection and analysis of the data with the intention of subsequent publication. This book is one of the main results.

The principal results of the Survey are here contained in carefully summarised form. An endeavour has been made not only to estab-

viii

lish an accurate record of damage from tree roots but also by defining the incidence of root damage more precisely than before to indicate the conditions under which trees might be planted near buildings with safety. Indeed, one of the main objectives of the Survey has always been not to prevent the planting of trees in built-up areas but to make easier the safe planting of trees in the neighbourhood of buildings.

I am confident that this book will prove of value as a source of authoritative guidance to the many people concerned with trees and buildings – arboriculturists, surveyors, architects, insurance representatives, those concerned with local government, etc. In this way I hope that trees as an element in the urban scene will increase without danger to the environment they help to beautify.

Professor J P M Brennan
*Director*

Royal Botanic Gardens
Kew, England
January 1981

# Preface to second edition

The first edition of this little book proved very popular and was reprinted several times. There has been an increasing demand for a revised edition with additional data. The first edition was based on research for the Kew Tree Root Survey. In preparing the second edition it was not possible to proceed in quite the same way. The extensive new information, from about 11 000 tree root and 1300 shrub root identifications, comes from Dr Richardson's laboratory records, and result from roots sent to him. No additional details could be collected on the distances of these trees and shrubs from the buildings they were thought to have damaged.

It is interesting to see that no changes occur in a 'league table' for trees that can cause damage to buildings as a result of the incorporation of the new figures. There is much improved information on the occurrence of roots in drains.

Many more shrub roots have been found in samples. It has become apparent that large shrubs and closely planted groups of shrubs can contribute to extensive soil drying. The section on shrubs has been enlarged in recognition of this, but it must be said that most shrubby species present only a slight danger, compared with the large, fast-growing trees. Some other new information has been incorporated in the hope that this will increase the usefulness of the book. This has been provided by Mr D Patch, and I am pleased to acknowledge his help. This includes notes on growth rates, the expected maximum age that trees may attain in an urban setting, the way they respond to pruning or lopping and other features of interest, for example whether or not they are liable to shed branches without warning.

Professor E A Bell
*Director*

Royal Botanic Gardens
Kew
November 1987

# Acknowledgements

Many individuals and professional bodies have provided advice, information and assistance, for which we are most grateful. The following have made particularly valuable contributions to the first or second editions:

Dr P G Biddle (Tree Conservation Ltd; text on clays), Dr W O Binns (Forestry Commission), Mr C D Brickell (Director General, Royal Horticultural Society), the British Insurance Association, Mr A G Burgess (formerly of Longstock Park Gardens), Mr R Driscoll (for the Building Research Establishment, DOE; text on foundations), Mr R G Grahame (Structural Engineer), Dr T Hall (for the Arboricultural Association), Mr D Harper (Loss Adjuster), Mr J Hayley (Great Gardens of England), The Institute of Loss Adjusters, Mr P Lardi (Structural Engineer), Professor F T Last (Institute of Terrestrial Ecology), Professor R Mead (University of Reading), Mr A Mitchell (formerly of Forestry Commission), Mr C R M Notcutt (Chairman and Managing Director, Notcutt's Nurseries), Mr D E Randall (For Institute of Landscape Architects), Dr E R C Reynolds (Plant Sciences Department, University of Oxford), the late Mr E Stevens (Harrington's, Builders) and Mr W E Storey (formerly of GLC Parks Department). We are also indebted to the Local Authorities and their officers who collaborated in supplying data on tree frequencies. We wish to acknowledge the encouragement and facilities given by the late Professor J P M Brennan, former Director of Kew, and the immediate past Director of Kew, Professor E A Bell. Mrs R M O Gale has spent a lot of time extracting data from the new records, contributing extensively to the production of this second edition.

Much valuable new information has been provided by Mr D Patch and his colleagues at the Forestry Commission and our special thanks are due to them.

# Chapter 1

# Introduction

## Scope and purpose

The data collected in the Kew Tree Root Survey (1971–79), and supplementary information concerned with the spread of roots from trees reported as having caused or contributed to damage to buildings, together with new data resulting from the business practice of Dr I B K Richardson, are presented in this book.

A very high proportion of all reported cases of such damage to buildings in Britain has probably occurred in the period of the survey and up to the present. During this time there has been an increase in public awareness of the problem, partly because of the introduction of subsidence cover to domestic policies by the major insurance companies, and the unusually extreme climatic conditions that included the 1975–76 drought.

Part of the information given in the entries for different types of tree was published in the first edition of this book. Additional data are incorporated from recent root identification work involving upwards of 11 000 trees. Shrubs may play a more important role in instances of damage to buildings than was previously supposed, and information on about 1300 shrub root identifications is also included. Often shrub roots and tree roots were found together in trial holes dug near to sites of damage. Root spread figures are taken from actual measurements.

There has been a growing acceptance of the significance of roots of trees and shrubs in certain problems of damage to buildings. It must be said here that root spread represents just one factor in the complex relationship between trees and buildings. A list of some of the additional factors to be considered is given in Chapter 2.

It is hoped that this information will be used by those whose work is concerned with trees and buildings, so that intelligent planting can be carried out in the future and more informed consideration given to the effects of retaining, or removing, trees that already beautify

1

our towns and cities. It should also help householders interested in maintaining or increasing garden tree planting with a minimum of risk to their own or their neighbour's property.

# The Kew Tree Root Survey

Up to 1970 very little had been written about the root systems of trees commonly planted in streets and gardens. Most of the information available related to trees as commercial forest crops, or to fruit trees. It is extremely difficult to obtain information on root systems, and the investigation of enough trees by excavation for general ideas to be formulated about rooting behaviour is out of the question both in terms of time and cost. However, early in the 1970s we realised that, if trial holes had to be dug to look for roots in order to establish the identity and probable ownership of a tree allegedly contributing to damage of a building, at least part of the work was done. Useful information with wider implications could thus be obtained quickly and inexpensively.

It was evident that people were overreacting to the possibility of trees damaging buildings. So-called 'safe planting distances' in use at that time were based on too little information.

Since the Jodrell Laboratory at Kew was already involved with the anatomical identification of roots, it was decided in 1971 to expand investigations by launching the Kew Tree Root Survey. This was initiated as a joint project with arboriculturists at Kew, greatly encouraged by the Arboricultural Association and others concerned with trees. A wealth of data was accumulated during succeeding years from the many who were willing to provide information on a simple survey card when they had to remove trees or when trial holes were dug to provide roots for identification.

Reference has already been made (p. 1) to the source of a considerable amount of new data obtained since the Kew Tree Root Survey was completed, and which are incorporated into this edition.

## Soil movement and tree roots

Changes in volume occur in most clay soils as their water content alters; shrinking takes place as the soil dries out; in some types this is greater than in others. This may be compounded when active roots further dry the soil, producing local differential soil shrinkage. If shrinkage occurs under some types of foundation it may lead to building movement and structural failure. Foundations on most other types of soil, except some peats, are not at risk from this type of soil movement. The reverse of shrinkage (expansion, heave), was recorded less frequently as a cause of damage during the period of the survey. In recent years the problem of heave has become more widely recognised, particularly in association with the recovery of soils after the removal of dead elm trees. There have been additional instances of heave when building work was instituted on old orchard sites before the soil had recovered to its normal field water capacity.

When it is suspected that heave rather than soil shrinkage is the cause of damage, examination of tree roots from the soil for signs of life is invaluable in reaching sound conclusions. The most certain results are obtained when the excavated roots can be identified as not belonging to neighbouring trees, but to those previously removed from the site. Live roots, with starch reserves, stain blue with the iodine test. Dead roots, still showing structure but lacking starch, do not stain blue with this test. The presence of live roots from previously removed trees could well indicate that the soil has not had time to re-hydrate fully.

Existing properties have been damaged in a similar way by removal of large trees near to them. The clay soil in these instances expanded as it reabsorbed moisture. Consequently more attention needs to be paid to the possibility of heave following the removal of trees.

During the period 1984–85, the following records were made by the Sun Alliance Insurance Group, for claims directly due to trees:

(a) heave – 1 out of 22 notified cases;
(b) landslip – 1 out of 20 notified cases;
(c) subsidence – 57 out of 683 notified cases.

This helps to put the risk of heave into perspective.

The reader is referred to BRE *Digest 298* for further information. Care should be taken when following the advice it contains for pruning. Total crown volume (hence leaf area) is generally more important than absolute height in relation to water demand. We have included data on the pruning response for various types of tree in this edition. It should also be borne in mind that regular pruning will be necessary to maintain a particular crown volume.

Any pruning may increase vulnerability to fungal diseases which can weaken a tree. The employment of professionals for heavy pruning is advised.

Another category of tree damage is drain blockage by root penetration of leaking drains, sometimes resulting in bursting of the drain, cavitation of the soil and subsequent foundation failure. Settlement may also be caused by local wetting of a clay soil; leaking drains can seriously affect the load-bearing capacity of clays,

3

particularly on sloping sites. Escaped water from drains may itself be enough to cause problems to foundations but a combination of root drying of soil below one part of a foundation and excessive wetting from a drain in another part is a recipe for disaster.

Direct mechanical damage by large roots causing pressure on a building or wall was rarely reported to us. Its effects are often local and the causes are usually very obvious. This problem is further discussed in the BSI *Code of Practice for Trees in Relation to Construction* (1980). There are occasional reports of damage from roots beneath foundations that have caused movement because of wind-rocking of the whole tree.

## Tree height

Since tree height is easy to estimate, it is natural for the layperson to wish to make predictions of root spread from height figures alone. There has been pressure on us to include more information on the relationship between root spread and tree height in this revised edition. Unfortunately this can be done only with limited accuracy from the information to hand, and may therefore be misleading.

The actual or attainable height of a tree has significance in an urban setting. For large trees the effects of shade, branches brushing buildings and the potential for certain of them to drop branches are all important factors to be considered. It is less clear how height and potential for root damage to buildings are related. For example, vigorous, semi-mature trees with a very active root system may be drawing on water from the soil more effectively and in greater quantities than taller, old trees well past their prime.

# The original data
## The survey card

Figure 1.1 shows a survey card. It was designed after discussions with officers at the Forestry Commission Research Station, Alice Holt, and in consultation with the MAFF Organization and Methods Section. Cards were issued to members of the professions dealing with trees, primarily those sending roots for identification at Kew (loss adjusters, surveyors, structural engineers, arboriculturists and so on). Nearly 3000 cards were returned to Kew; about 2600 of them that had been completed adequately were considered for this publication. Other, extensive data were also available (see p. 8). Most of the returns came from London and the South-East, a fact which must be related in part at least to the high incidence of shrinkable clay soils in those regions, and the building density.

TREE ROOT SURVEY
ROYAL BOTANIC GARDENS, KEW, RICHMOND, SURREY

FOR USE AT KEW
A.A.D.P.D. PUNCH

| | | |
|---|---|---|
| 1 | | |
| 2 | | |
| 3 | | |
| 4 | | |
| 5 | | |
| 6 | | |
| 7 | | |
| 8 | | |
| 9 | | |
| 10 | | |
| 11 | | |
| 12 | | |
| 13 M | | |
| 13 YR | | |

1. Tree Species:

2. Variety or Form:

3. Height (m) | 4. Root Spread (RADIAL)
3-6 m   7-8 m   9-10 m   11-12 m   13-15 m   16-20 m   If >20 m state spread

5. If roots severed give diameter of thickest broken ends ........ cm

6. Soil Type:

7. Tree Position:   Solitary

8. Tree was:   Diseased   Blown Down

In Avenue   In Stand   Damaging Building   Drive   Wall

9. Root Type   lateral   tap and lateral   lateral and droppers

10. Distance from building, drive or wall (if appropriate – see 8) ........ m.

11. Depth of soil over solid barrier (if any) ........ cm

12. Location of Tree:   Name of Town   County

13. Name ........................ (block capitals please)
    Date ........................

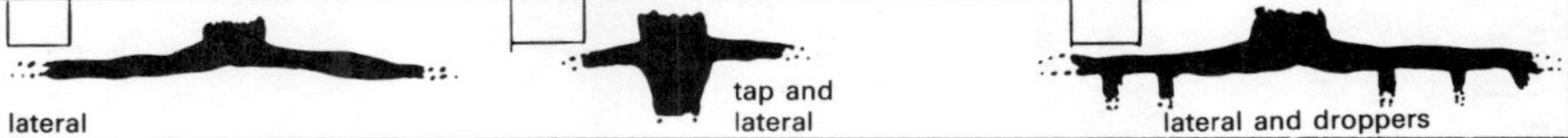

*Figure 1.1 A survey card.*

5

The boxes on the card are mainly self-explanatory, but they are discussed below in relation to the information supplied.

*Box 1, 2. Name of tree, variety or form.* Identification of the roots provided this information for the enquirer to complete. Consequently the limitations of the ability to make some particular identifications are reflected here. For example, because poplar and willow roots cannot be distinguished from one another with any degree of certainty, all such roots were identified as from *Salicaceae*, the family to which both groups belong. Many cards would consequently have the tree identification to the family level only, although those completing the cards often revisited the site and determined whether the tree was a poplar or willow and gave the additional information.

No extra site data were available for *Acer* species where all the Acers have to be grouped together regardless of whether they were sycamores or maples.

In the accounts which follow in Chapter 3, the notes indicate for different types of tree the ease or difficulty in distinguishing between the species from their root structure.

*Box 3. Height of tree.* Many of those completing the cards were professionals, used to estimating heights and distances. Since the trees were for the most part in urban situations it was possible to use nearby buildings as a scale, for example, about 3 m to each storey.

It was anticipated that heights would be rounded off. When the survey was started, measurements were entered in feet, and there were clear clusterings in the height records such as 30, 40 and 50 feet. These did not exactly match the equivalent clusters recorded on the later, metric cards. Popular categories were then 10, 12, 15 metres and so on. This reinforces our view that the height data must be considered as rough estimates only, individual differences of one metre certainly being insignificant.

*Box 4. Radial root spread.* Seven distance categories are given. The returns for this box were used for trees which were isolated from buildings – e.g. trees blown down in open spaces. Normally when box 10 was also completed (distance from building, drive or wall) the measurements given there were accepted as more accurate, as they had not been fitted into distance categories as for box 4.

*Box 5. Diameter of roots.* Returns soon indicated that roots do not taper at an even rate, so that their thickness gives little indication of the distance that they might extend from the point of measurement. One of the original objectives was to estimate root taper rate from this information, and that had to be abandoned.

*Box 6.  Soil type.* Nearly 95 per cent of the cards returned related to subsidence damage cases on clay soils. The remaining 5 per cent were for fallen trees or drain damage on other types of soil. A subdivision of the types of clay is not possible from the information returned in box 6, but some indication can be obtained indirectly by reference to the locality of the building (box 12) or from our enquiry records, together with examination of the soil maps (see p. 9).

*Box 7.  Tree position.* Various people interpreted the categories in different ways. There was little ambiguity when a tree was solitary or in a group. In an avenue of widely spaced trees it is possible for smaller species to be regarded as solitary by some or in an avenue by others. With this possibility of confusion it was decided not to use these results in this report. The analyses showed no differences between the root spread of trees in the various associations though some were expected, e.g. National House Building Council Practice Note 3 (1974) recommended deeper foundations where trees near to buildings are in rows or groups, but this advice was dropped later in NHBC Practice Note 3, (1985 [1986]).

*Box 8.  Tree condition and nature of damage.* Almost all the cards showed that some structural damage was involved in the enquiry. The great majority related to damage to buildings. The records of diseased or wind-blown trees will be considered in further articles.

*Box 9.  Root type.* At the outset few people were expected to be able to obtain this information because excavations were rarely made near to the base of the tree. However, such information as was returned showed that the type consisting of lateral roots only was the most common, but droppers (vertical roots) were also found on occasions in almost every type of tree. Tap roots are normally broken when transplants are made, thus the original tap root would not be present unless the tree germinated on site.

*Box 10.  Distance from building, drive or wall.* See under box 4.

*Box 11.  Depth of soil over solid barrier.* It was hoped that rooting behaviour in shallow soils and in-filled sites could have been considered. The box was rarely completed.

*Box 12. Location of tree.* This was used for mapping the distribution of root damage and was supplemented by information from other sources.

# Other sources of data

*Roots and building damage.* Although the largest proportion of the data presented in this book stems from the Kew Tree Root Survey Cards, several other sources of data have contributed important information.

Reference has already been made to some of these. Among them are the records at Kew of about 7000 inspection holes dug when it was suspected that trees might be involved in damage. They include the 2600 root identifications for which there are cards. New records from 11 000 tree roots and 2300 shrub roots compiled by I B K Richardson are incorporated in the analyses. Relevant data usually comprise the address of the property and the identity of the roots submitted. Further data on the location of enquiries were kindly provided by the Building Research Establishment. The map shown in Figure 1.2 giving the percentage incidence of root enquiries for various areas in South East England was constructed from these data.

*Species planting frequencies.* As previously mentioned, the data from the survey cards and identifications are almost entirely derived from instances where the trees concerned are thought to have been involved in some form of building damage.

This was sufficient to enable a preliminary assessment to be made of the relative frequency with which a particular tree type contributed to structural damage, but to this must be added some estimate of the relative number of trees of each type planted in urban settings. This would give a more accurate indication of the likelihood of a particular type to damage buildings, since planting frequency could itself influence the frequency of damage. Surveys to obtain this sort of information are costly and difficult to make, and become highly impractical when back-garden as well as street and front-garden plantings are concerned. However, as a compromise solution to this problem we were most grateful to receive street tree planting figures involving a total of 39 500 trees from seven Local Authorities (three of which are in the London clay area), whilst Mr J Hayley (Great Gardens of England) and Mr C R M Notcutt of Notcutts Nurseries very kindly gave us access to sales figures for selected

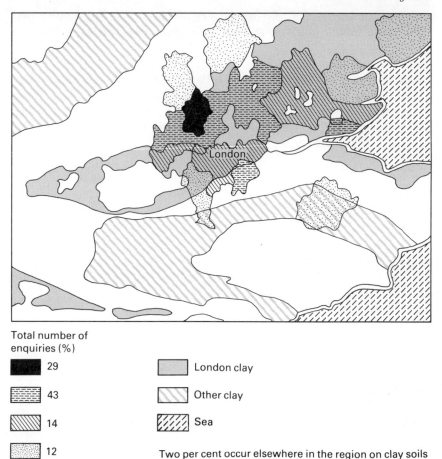

Total number of
enquiries (%)

| | | | |
|---|---|---|---|
| ■ 29 | | London clay | |
| 43 | | Other clay | |
| 14 | | Sea | |
| 12 | | Two per cent occur elsewhere in the region on clay soils | |

*Figure 1.2 Incidence of enquiries from various areas of South East England (%)*

types of trees, a number greatly exceeding that from the Local Authorities.

It must be stressed that great care should be exercised when predicting, even from such large numbers.

*Tree dimensions.* What can be termed the 'normal maximum height' of trees, as opposed to that attained in the rural environment, has been supplied for each entry by Mr A F Mitchell, a former member of the Forestry Commission staff who is renowned for his knowledge on tree dimensions in Britain. Dr W O Binns, also of the Forestry Commission, has provided us with tentative information on the

9

depth of rooting systems for some trees on clay soils. This is included as a guide in the notes at the end of certain tree entries.

*Response to pruning and other tree features.* Not all trees can be pruned or pollarded satisfactorily. Mr D Patch, and colleagues, Forestry Commission, have provided data on response to pruning and crown management, and notes on other characteristics of various species, for example the production of undesirable exudation, or the propensity to shed limbs.

## Chapter 2
# Trees and other site factors

In the introduction reference has been made to the many factors, in addition to trees, which may cause structural failure in a building. For example the figures given by Reece (1979) show that trees were considered to have been involved to some extent in 2285 claims in a total of 10 684 subsidence cases. Of the 2285 claims, 88 per cent arose from a combination of clay and tree roots, but the other 12 per cent were due to a combination of trees and additional factors.

With the assistance of a number of specialists the following account has been prepared which considers how best to determine the factors involved in damage. It is included at the request of many of the potential users. The list is not a complete one but reference can be made to Biddle (1979) for further information. The extent of damage will determine how far one should follow up each point, bearing in mind the costs involved.

## The trees

(a)   Excavations should be made at the site of damage, and, where soil shrinkage is observed close to the foundations, roots looked for. For legal purposes, roots must be found and identified before particular trees can be implicated. The size of the roots, a rough indication of their frequency, and whether they appear live or dead, should be noted.

(b)   A map should be drawn showing the distribution, identity and size of all trees and shrubs which could be implicated. The root-spread figures recorded in this book can be used to assist with this.

The effects tree roots may have can be modified by the position of the trees around the building. For example, trees to one side only, or at a corner, could have a marked effect because their soil drying pattern would be localised.

Some specialists have observed that the trees nearest to a building with subsidence damage are not necessarily those which have contributed to that damage.

The complex interaction between roots of trees of different species or between trees and shrubs is not yet understood.

(c)   Trees should be examined for evidence of pollarding or extensive crown thinning.

Trees of some species which are allowed to grow without further restrictions after severe pollarding can make large demands on soil water, and could upset a balance which had developed between the pollarded trees and buildings.

(d)   The general health and vigour of the trees should be noted. Healthy, vigorous trees of a particular species are likely to make more demand on water resources than those of equivalent height which are diseased or senescent.

(e)   Tree preservation orders may apply to some of the trees; no work should be done on them before this possibility is investigated.

(f)   Evidence of removal of trees should be looked for. Examination of earlier aerial photographs, for example, may help.

Volume change in the soil could have been due to expansion after the removal of trees rather than shrinkage.


# The soil

(g)   The soil type and its shrinkability must be determined. Soils vary in their ability to shrink. The majority of soils show insignificant dimensional changes with a change in moisture content, and it is almost entirely with the clay soils and some very peaty soils that shrinkage can become a problem. Clay soils are defined by the proportion of particles smaller than $2\,\mu$m (0.002 mm) that they contain, and the nature of the minerals involved (see BRE *Digests 63, 64* and *67*). However, within this loose definition there can be enormous variation. In particular, the clay can vary in its mineralogical composition, particle size distribution and colloid content, cation exchange capacity and the percentage of non-shrinkable materials such as sand. Soil analysis figures should be based on examination of the total sample; stones are an important component and must not be removed prior to analysis.

There are many factors which influence the shrinkability of the clay. Unfortunately there is no simple direct method of measuring the shrinkage or swelling characteristics of a soil on site and indirect methods must be used.

The most widely used method is based on the plasticity index of the soil (Holtz 1959), as shown in Table 2.1, which is quite easy to measure. However, even if the clay soil does fall into a highly shrinkable category, there are other factors, such as soil structure, soil permeability and moisture availability, which can influence the depth and spread of roots.

Table 2.1

| Degree of expansion or shrinkage | Plasticity index | Colloid content % (<0.001 mm) | Shrinkage limit |
|---|---|---|---|
| Very high | >35 | >28 | <11 |
| High | 25–41 | 20–31 | 7–12 |
| Medium | 15–28 | 13–23 | 10–16 |
| Low | <18 | <15 | >15 |

From: Holtz, W G (1959).

The results of this present root survey indicate the need for defining shrinkability and soil type for each site. Figure 2.1 shows the geographical distribution of enquiries. 75 per cent of them originate from areas where the predominant soil type is London clay (but also where housing density is the greatest). Some of the remaining examples are from areas with shrinkable, and others non-shrinkable, soils, although the great majority are from soils marked as clay on the survey cards. This suggests that a few of the enquiries did not necessarily relate to problems of structural damage due to soil shrinkage. Special care must be taken on site to make a proper soil examination to minimise the risk of wrongly implicating trees. It would appear that clays other than London clay, although they may shrink, present less of a problem. They may be more permeable and replenishing ground-water flow may prevent the shrinkage from taking place except in extreme conditions.

(h)   Previous works on site. All locally available information should be sought on location of services, etc. Remains of old drainage systems, old foundations and other areas of disturbed soil should be looked for. They may result in differential soil movement on the site.

(i)   Locally wet areas. Natural sources of water or leaking drains can lead to locally wet areas of soil. Even in the absence of trees this could lead to uneven drying, and uneven shrinking in certain clay soils. If such sources of water are suspected, soil moisture content should be measured. Sometimes such ground water is the main source for established trees, and may help to prevent the tree from causing the development of local areas of dry soil. Clearly anything which reduces or removes such water supplies could result in a previously harmless tree drying a clay soil to a degree which causes shrinkage, and should be avoided both during new development and on sites with existing buildings.

# Buildings

(j)  Foundation type. If constructed before the 1950s low-rise buildings (up to and including 4 storeys) will frequently have foundations to a depth of only about 0.5 m though some are deeper. After this period foundation standards were improved, and depths increased to about 1 m. These existing buildings, especially the older ones, may be at risk from tree root activity in very dry weather should trees be growing or planted too close to the building. Houses with full basements or cellars below this depth are not so vulnerable.

For new low-rise buildings, foundation designs have been published to minimise building movement and damage on clay soils where volume changes due to tree root action can be expected (Building Research Establishment 1965, 1972, 1976; Tomlinson *et al.* 1978). Three specific situations have been recognised for new constructions:

  (i)  where buildings are erected close to existing trees;
 (ii)  where new trees are to be planted near new buildings;
(iii)  where trees are removed from a clay site to enable new construction to take place.

In situations (i) and (ii), for construction within the existing or future zone of influence of tree roots (depending on the development of the tree), foundations must be deep enough to extend into the soil where significant volume changes will not occur, even in extreme drought conditions. If the required depth exceeds about 1.5 m it will be sensible, for economic reasons, to consider adopting a small diameter pile and beam foundation which consists of concrete-filled, vertical, cylindrical holes drilled into the clay soil to depths up to about 4 m (depending on the depth of tree root influence). Greater depths may be required in some circumstances. The piles are connected at their heads by horizontal, reinforced concrete beams on which the walls are erected (see Tomlinson *et al.* (1978) for details). For the case of tree removal (situation (iii) ), substantial damage has been known to occur as a result of the swelling of clay

14

previously permanently dried by large trees (Samuels and Cheney 1974; Cheney and Burford 1974). In this situation it is essential to provide a stable foundation below the zone of dried soil, which has been known to extend to depths exceeding 4 m adjacent to some very large trees. Not only should reinforced pile foundations be adopted to prevent upward movement of the building, but beams and floor slabs should be suspended above ground so that the ground surface can heave without causing disruption, or flexible packing should be provided under the beams and slabs.

(k)   Type of construction materials. Certain types of building materials are less flexible than others and are more easily damaged by soil movement.

(l)   Extensions, porches and bays. The foundations of bays are often shallower than those of the rest of the structure. Extensions, porches and bays can be inadequately or incorrectly tied into the rest of the structure.

(m)   Backfill. Roots can exploit good growing conditions in loose backfill. Backfill for foundations or root barriers should be carried out on the side away from trees, or the soil should be compacted near the barrier.

# Aspect and immediate environment

(n)   Shading and degree of exposure to rain and sun can contribute towards differing moisture contents being present in the soil in various places around a building.

(o)   Impervious surfaces. These influence the soil moisture locally, and could cause roots to spread further than they would otherwise, or affect their direction.

(p)   Topography. This has effects on drainage and therefore soil moisture, as well as tree root growth. Extreme slopes and high water content can make some soils unstable.

(q)   Vibrations. Heavy traffic, trains and underground working can contribute to structural damage.

# Time of year

(r)   If damage occurs, the timetable of events should be carefully noted. In a normal (i.e. non-drought) year, the soil is progressively dried by tree roots in the summer months when net loss of water occurs despite wet periods of weather. If cracks first appear at the end of the summer, differential soil drying is to be suspected, and trees may possibly be implicated.

Most of the items described above need specialist interpretation for each individual case. As mentioned on p. 25, they are included as a general guide, in the hope that trees will not be needlessly condemned when other factors could have contributed substantially to subsidence damage.

*Figure 2.1 Cross-sections of roots as seen under the microscope. All are magnified × 45. The only safe way to identify small pieces of detached root is to make such preparations and compare them with authenticated reference collections.*
*Top: Rose, Rosa species. Centre: Sycamore, Acer pseudoplatanus. Bottom: Birch, Betula species. Details of the types of cell present and their distribution in the tissue have to be studied, both in cross-section and longitudinal section, to confirm an identification. The Root Identification manual of trees and shrubs. Cutler et al. (1987) contains 549 such photographs.*

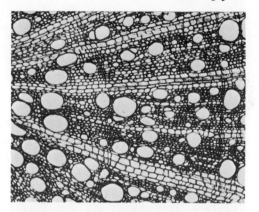

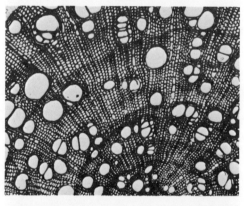

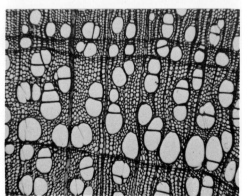

## Chapter 3

# Root spread of commonly planted trees in Britain

## Notes for use in conjunction with the tree entries

Trees which are commonly associated with building damage are each given a double page (pp. 24–55). Other trees which from time to time have been recorded to have caused damage to buildings have brief entries (pp. 57–61).

Conifers are considered on pp. 62–65, and shrubs on pp. 66–67.

The entries are concise, and need some explanation so that they may be interpreted satisfactorily. The following notes should be read in conjunction with the data. It is particularly important that all the relevant variables should be considered in each investigation.

## Hypothetical figures to act as an example, for 'species A'

TREE NAME in English, followed by scientific equivalent – 'species A'; sometimes the rooting habit of only one species is described; more often several species from a closely related group have to be taken together because they cannot be distinguished by anatomical structure of the roots (see p. 6).

(1) Maximum tree-to-damage distance recorded for hypothetical 'species A': 20 m.

This figure represents the extreme for our data. Often only a very small proportion, less than 5 per cent, of our records for the species would be near to this maximum.

In 90 per cent of the cases the tree 'species A' was closer than 10 m.

(2) Normal maximum height of 'species A' in shrinkable clay urban areas: 25 m.

This gives the best guide to the height usually attainable in the urban environment on shrinkable clay soils when the tree has not been severely pruned or lopped. It is generally less than that known for the same species growing in ideal field conditions.

This information will help those wishing to select trees for sites where shading and space availability are important considerations, and where foundations are suitably constructed so that root problems can be discounted.

(3) Percentage of cases of damage occurring within certain bands of distance from the tree 'species A' on shrinkable clay soils.

| Cases of damage (%) | Distance from damage (m) |
| --- | --- |
| 0 | Over 20 |
| 10 | 10–20 |
| 15 | 8–10 |
| 25 | 6–8 |
| 25 | 3–6 |
| 25 | 0–3 |

Fixed percentage proportions for tree damage are given for all species (left-hand column). For each of these figures the relevant distances are given for the particular species (right-hand column). This enables comparisons between species to be made readily, since the distances are the variables, and not the percentage of damage reported.

In the example cited above, no damage is recorded for trees more than 20 m from buildings, 90 per cent occurred within 10 m of buildings, 75 per cent occurred within 8 m, and so on.

(4) Figure 3.1 is a graph showing the reduction in percentage of cases of damage recorded as the distance of trees of 'species A' from buildings increases (for shrinkable clay soils).

Graphs are used to supplement the distance band data given under (3). Each is started from the distance within which 50 per cent of damage cases were recorded for the particular species.

Histograms representing a 2-metre increment were used in the construction of the graphs and best-fit curves drawn. The graphs are thus approximate, but give a good guide for comparison of the root spread of different sorts of tree.

Elm, oak, poplar and willow have a high proportion of cases of damage recorded at long distances from the trees. The scale on the

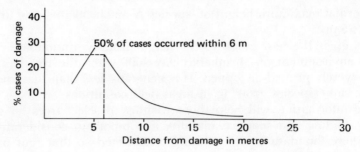

*Root spread of commonly planted trees in Britain*

50% of cases occurred within 6 m

% cases of damage

Distance from damage in metres

*Figure 3.1*

per cent (vertical) axis is doubled for these to make the graphs easier to read.

From Fig. 3.1, for 'species A' it can be seen for example that at 10 m, 7 per cent of cases of damage by that species were recorded.

(5a) Percentage of tree 'species A', relative to the total for all trees reported to have caused damage: 5 per cent.
(5b) Estimated percentage of tree 'species A' used in street and garden planting: 2 per cent.

(5a) This figure represents the percentage of the particular species occurring in our sample of 7000.
(5b) This figure is derived from (i) data provided by local authorities from plantings on soils which are mainly of the shrinkable clay type; the sample size is 39 500 (of which London Boroughs contribute 22 300) and (ii) much more extensive data from suppliers of trees.

In this example, then, 'species A' is found to be involved in damage at a rate above that which would be expected for its representation in plantings. If all other factors were equal, one might expect incidence of damage to relate closely to planting frequency for a species.

The nature of the information examined did not allow a satisfactory statistical analysis to be made, but the percentages can be used to indicate trends where figures (5a) and (5b) are widely different.

(6) Percentage of cases of damage by 'species A' involving shrinkable clay soils: 98 per cent.

Very little damage is reported from trees on other than shrinkable clays. The considerations for planting trees close to buildings on non-shrinkable soils would relate mainly to the ultimate size of the

20

tree, convenience, e.g. shade, available space, the type of fruits, sticky deposits and so on.

(7) Sample number: 116 cards, 420 additional identifications.

(8) Proportion of cases of tree damage to drains involving 'species A': 5 per cent.

Our original sample for drain damage overall (41 out of 7000 samples) was very low, but this does not represent the true picture. In most instances the cause of drain damage was so obvious as to need no identification work. The new data incorporated in this edition have improved the accuracy of these figures.

Insurance Companies deal with as many claims of drain damage as cases of subsidence.

It is important to remember that different sources of information were used to provide the data in this book. In each of the main descriptions, items 1, 3, 4 and 6 contain figures derived from card returns. Data in (5a) and (8) were extracted from the records in the Anatomy Laboratory enquiry book and from Ian Richardson's new records. Identifications listed in (7) also contain the new records.

The notes give additional information, much of which was provided by Mr D Patch and colleagues from the Forestry Commission.

The life expectancy figures provide a general guide. Diseased trees or those growing in adverse conditions may not live as long, or may become unsafe well before they reach the ages indicated. For timing of pruning or crown thinning the reader should consult a local arboriculturist.

# The tree entries

# APPLE   *Malus* species (fruit trees and ornamentals)

# PEAR   *Pyrus* species

1. Maximum tree-to-damage distance recorded: 10 m. In 90 per cent of cases the tree was closer than 8 m.
2. Normal maximum height in shrinkable clay urban areas: apple: 8–10 m, pear: 12 m.
3. Proportion of cases of damage occurring within certain bands of distance from the tree species on shrinkable clay soils:

| Cases of damage (%) | Distance from damage (m) |
|---|---|
| 0 | Over 10 |
| 10 | 8–10 |
| 15 | 6–8 |
| 25 | 4–6 |
| 25 | 3–4 |
| 25 | 0.1–3 |

4. Figure 3.2 is a graph showing the reduction in percentage of cases of damage recorded as the distance of trees from buildings increases (for shrinkable clay soils).

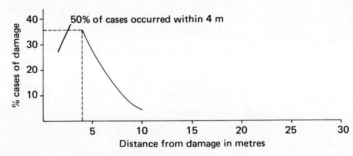

*Figure 3.2*

5a. Percentage of apple and pear trees relative to the total for all trees reported to have caused damage: *c.* 5.7 per cent.
5b. Estimated percentage of apple and pear trees used in street and garden planting relative to sample figures for all such tree plantings: 7.1 per cent.
6. Percentage of cases of damage by apple and pear trees involving shrinkable clay soils: 96 per cent.

7.  Sample number: 80 cards, 678 additional identifications (including some shrubs).
8.  Apple and pear trees were involved in 2.0 per cent of all cases of tree damage to drains recorded.

*Notes:* Apple, pear, hawthorn and *Sorbus* tree roots can all be confused with one another. These trees are closely related and belong to the group Pomoideae. Further problems of identification of roots can arise because grafting is commonly practised with members of this group.

The sample of 80 represents 61 cases definitely attributable to apple and 19 to pear; other samples could not be included in the analysis. In the new data the 678 specimens were not identified to genus, but include the shrubs *Chaenomeles, Cotoneaster, Cydonia* and *Pyracantha*.

Apples and pears are shallow-rooted, locally deep. Growth rate is medium under good conditions. Life expectancy is generally under 50 years. Both young and old trees will tolerate light pruning. Some trees are prone to suckering and growth of twigs around the trunk base. Many varieties are vulnerable to aphids. Fire blight may be a problem.

# ASH  *Fraxinus* species

1. Maximum tree-to-damage distance recorded: 21 m. In 90 per cent of cases the tree was closer than 13 m.
2. Normal maximum height in shrinkable clay urban areas: *Fraxinus excelsior*, common ash: 23 m, *F. ornus*, manna or flowering ash: 14 m.
3. Proportion of cases of damage occurring within certain bands of distance from the tree species on shrinkable clay soils:

| *Cases of damage (%)* | *Distance from damage (m)* |
|---|---|
| 0 | Over 21 |
| 10 | 13–21 |
| 15 | 10–13 |
| 25 | 6–10 |
| 25 | 4–6 |
| 25 | 1–4 |

4. Figure 3.3 is a graph showing the reduction in percentage of cases of damage recorded as the distance of trees from buildings increases (for shrinkable clay soils).

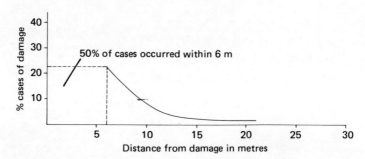

*Figure 3.3*

5a. Percentage of ash trees relative to the total for all trees reported to have caused damage: 7.5 per cent.
5b. Estimated percentage of ash trees used in street and garden planting relative to sample figures for all such tree plantings: 3 per cent.
6. Percentage of cases of damage by ash trees involving shrinkable clay soils: more than 99 per cent.

26

7.   Sample number:145 cards; 862 additional identifications.
8.   Ash trees were involved in 4.5 per cent of all cases of tree damage to drains recorded.

*Notes:* Species of ash cannot be distinguished from each other on root structure alone; some are grafted.

Ashes can be deep-rooted on clay soils. Growth rate is fast under good conditions. Life expectancy can be over 100 years. Both young and old trees will tolerate heavy pruning and crown reduction.

Ashes tend to form weak upright forks, and are prone to branch shedding. The leaves are poisonous to livestock. Some species fruit freely and the resultant seedlings may cause problems. Root damage may result in susceptibility to disease.

# BEECH  *Fagus* species

1.  Maximum tree-to-damage distance recorded: 15 m. In 90 per cent of cases the tree was closer than 11 m.
2.  Normal maximum height in shrinkable clay urban areas: 20 m.
3.  Proportion of cases of damage occurring within certain bands of distance from the three species on shrinkable clay soils:

| Cases of damage (%) | Distance from damage (m) |
|:---:|:---:|
| 0 | Over 15 |
| 10 | 11–15 |
| 15 | 9–11 |
| 25 | 6–9 |
| 25 | 2–6 |
| 25 | 0.7–2 |

4.  Figure 3.4 is a graph showing the reduction in percentage of cases of damage recorded as the distance of trees from buildings increases (for shrinkable clay soils).

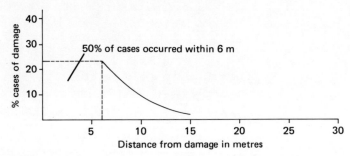

*Figure 3.4*

5a. Percentage of beech trees relative to the total for all trees reported to have caused damage: less than 1 per cent.
5b. Estimated percentage of beech trees used in street and garden planting relative to sample figures for all such tree plantings: about 1 per cent.
6.  Percentage of cases of damage by beech trees involving shrinkable clay soils: 100 per cent.
7.  Sample number: 23 cards; 131 additional identifications.
8.  Beech trees were involved in less than 1 per cent of all cases of tree damage to drains recorded.

*Notes:* Beeches are scarce on clay as they require free drainage.
They are shallow-rooted on clay soils.

Growth rate is fast in good conditions. Life expectancy can be over 100 years. Young trees will tolerate heavy pruning, and old trees, light pruning. Some specimens produce weak upright forks. Branch shedding may be a problem and entire trees may become unstable in old age as a result of major root rot.

# BIRCH  *Betula* species

1. Maximum tree-to-damage distance recorded: 10 m. In 90 per cent of cases the tree was closer than 8 m.
2. Normal maximum height in shrinkable clay urban areas: 12–14 m.
3. Proportion of cases of damage occurring within certain bands of distance from the three species on shrinkable clay soils:

| Cases of damage (%) | Distance from damage (m) |
|:---:|:---:|
| 0 | Over 10 |
| 10 | 8–10 |
| 15 | 7–8 |
| 25 | 4–7 |
| 25 | 3–4 |
| 25 | 1.5–3 |

4. Figure 3.5 is a graph showing the reduction in percentage of cases of damage recorded as the distance of trees from buildings increases (for shrinkable clay soils).

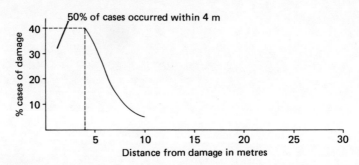

*Figure 3.5*

5a. Percentage of birch trees relative to the total for all trees reported to have caused damage: 1.5 per cent.
5b. Estimated percentage of birch trees used in street and garden planting relative to sample figures for all such tree plantings: 4.9 per cent.
6. Percentage of cases of damage by birch trees involving shrinkable clay soils: 100 per cent.
7. Sample number: 35 cards; 182 additional identifications.
8. Birch trees were involved in 5.5 per cent of all cases of tree damage to drains recorded.

*Notes: Betula* species cannot be distinguished from each other on root structure alone. However, *B. pendula* is rare on clay so it is probable that most cases relate to *B. pubescens*, although a few of the more ornamental species and varieties could have been involved. Birch is shallow-rooted on clay soils.

Growth rate is medium in good conditions. Life expectancy is between 50 and 100 years. Free fruiting, can become a weed. Young trees will tolerate heavy pruning, but older trees only light pruning.

# CHERRIES, PLUMS, DAMSONS, etc
*Prunus* species

1. Maximum tree-to-damage distance recorded: 11 m. In 90 per cent of cases the tree was closer than 7.5 m.
2. Normal maximum height in shrinkable clay urban areas: the largest flowering cherries may reach 12 m, but many *Prunus* species attain only 6–8 m.
3. Proportion of cases of damage occurring within certain bands of distance from the three species on shrinkable clay soils:

| Cases of damage (%) | Distance from damage (m) |
|:---:|:---:|
| 0 | Over 11 |
| 10 | 7.5–11 |
| 15 | 6–7.5 |
| 25 | 3–6 |
| 25 | 2–3 |
| 25 | 1–2 |

4. Figure 3.6 is a graph showing the reduction in percentage of cases of damage recorded as the distance of trees from buildings increases (for shrinkable clay soils).

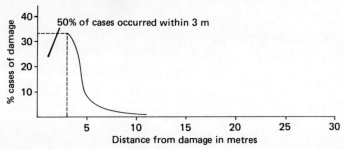

*Figure 3.6*

5a. Percentage of *Prunus* trees relative to the total for all trees reported to have caused damage: 6.4 per cent.
5b. Estimated percentage of *Prunus* trees used in street and garden planting relative to sample figures for all such tree plantings: 14.7 per cent.
6. Percentage of cases of damage by *Prunus* trees involving shrinkable clay soils: 100 per cent.
7. Sample number: 114 cards; 746 additional identifications (including some shrubs).

32

8.  *Prunus* trees were involved in 4.5 per cent of all cases of tree damage to drains recorded.

*Notes: Prunus* species cannot be distinguished from each other on root structure alone. Roots of the shrubs cherry-laurel (*Prunus laurocerasus*) and Portugal laurel (*P. lusitanicus*) are included in the sample number.

Roots of *Prunus* species are shallow to moderately deep on clay soils.

Growth rate is medium in good conditions. Life expectancy is less than 50 years. Both young and old trees will tolerate only light pruning. Some species are free fruiting and may be a nuisance. The shallow rooting habit can be a problem in mown grass, where injury to the roots may induce suckering.

# ELM  *Ulmus* species

1. Maximum tree-to-damage distance recorded: 25 m. In 90 per cent of cases the tree was closer than 19 m.
2. Normal maximum height in shrinkable clay urban areas: *Ulmus procera:* 25 m, *U. glabra:* 17–20, *U. carpinifolia* 'Sarniensis': 20–24 m.
3. Proportion of cases of damage occurring within certain bands of distance from the tree species on shrinkable clay soils:

| Cases of damage (%) | Distance from damage (m) |
|---|---|
| 0 | Over 25 |
| 10 | 19–25 |
| 15 | 12–19 |
| 25 | 8–12 |
| 25 | 5.5–8 |
| 25 | 1–5.5 |

4. Figure 3.7 is a graph showing the reduction in percentage of cases of the damage recorded as the distance of trees from buildings increases (for shrinkable clay soils).

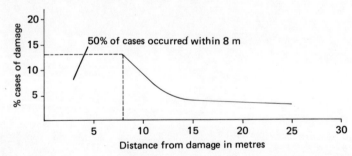

*Figure 3.7*

5. Most of the enquiries related to elm trees which were dead or dying. They represented about 2 per cent of trees reported to have caused damage. No data were available for planting frequency.
6. Percentage of cases of damage by elm trees involving shrinkable clay soils: 100 per cent.
7. Sample number: 70 cards; 246 additional identifications.
8. Elm trees were involved in less than 1 per cent of all cases of tree damage to drains recorded.

*Notes*: Species of elm cannot be distinguished from each other on root structure alone.

Elms can have deep roots on clay soils.

Growth rate is fast in good conditions. Most species are vulnerable to Dutch Elm Disease and aphid attack. Life expectancy is over 100 years for undiseased trees. Elms may shed branches without warning, and are prone to suckering. Both young and old trees tolerate heavy pruning or crown thinning. It is not yet known whether regrowths from hedges following Dutch Elm Disease will survive.

# FALSE ACACIA  *Robinia* species

1. Maximum tree-to-damage distance recorded: 12.4 m. In 90 per cent of cases the tree was closer than 10.5 m.
2. Normal maximum height in shrinkable clay urban areas: 18–20 m.
3. Proportion of cases of damage occurring within certain bands of distance from the tree species on shrinkable clay soils:

| Cases of damage (%) | Distance from damage (m) |
|---|---|
| 0 | Over 12.4 |
| 10 | 10.5–12.4 |
| 15 | 8.5–10.5 |
| 25 | 7–8.5 |
| 25 | 4–7 |
| 25 | 2–4 |

4. Figure 3.8 is a graph showing the reduction in percentage of cases of damage recorded as the distance of trees from buildings increases (for shrinkable clay soils).

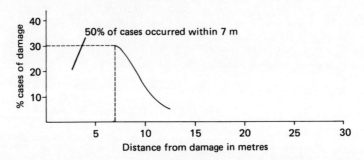

*Figure 3.8*

5a. Percentage of *Robinia* trees relative to the total for all trees reported to have caused damage: 3 per cent.
5b. Estimated percentage of *Robinia* trees used in street and garden planting relative to sample figures for all such tree plantings: 1.8 per cent.
6. Percentage of cases of damage by *Robinia* trees involving shrinkable clay soils: 100 per cent.
7. Sample number: 20 cards; 391 additional identifications, some of which are for *Laburnum*.

36

8.   *Robinia* trees were involved in less than 1 per cent of all cases of damage to drains recorded.

*Notes: Robinia* trees are fast growing, and many specimens have yet to reach a large size. They can sucker profusely, and also produce prickly, brittle shoots.

Life expectancy is between 50 and 100 years. Young trees can be heavily pruned, but older trees tolerate only light pruning. They are prone to shed branches.

Roots of *Robinia* can be confused with those of *Laburnum, Sophora* and *Gleditsia* (see brief tree entries).

# HAWTHORN   *Crataegus* species

1.  Maximum tree-to-damage distance recorded: 11.5 m. In 90 per cent of cases the tree was closer than 8.7 m.
2.  Normal maximum height in shrinkable clay urban areas: 10 m.
3.  Proportion of cases of damage occurring within certain bands of distance from the tree species on shrinkable clay soils:

| *Cases of damage (%)* | *Distance from damage (m)* |
|---|---|
| 0 | Over 11.5 |
| 10 | 8.7–11.5 |
| 15 | 7–8.7 |
| 25 | 5–7 |
| 25 | 3–5 |
| 25 | 0.4–3 |

4.  Figure 3.9 is a graph showing the reduction in percentage of cases of damage recorded as the distance of trees from buildings increases (for shrinkable clay soils).

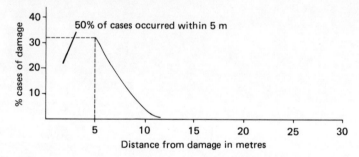

*Figure 3.9*

5a. Percentage of hawthorn trees relative to the total for all trees reported to have caused damage: 4.6 per cent.
5b. Estimated percentage of hawthorn trees used in street and garden planting relative to sample figures for all such tree plantings: 3.5 per cent.
6.  Percentage of cases of damage by hawthorn trees involving shrinkable clay soils: more than 99 per cent.
7.  Sample number: 65 cards; 550 additional identifications.
8.  Hawthorn trees were involved in 1.6 per cent of all cases of damage to drains recorded.

*Notes*: Roots of hawthorn species can be confused with those from apple, pear and *Sorbus* trees. The sample number of 65 represents cases definitely attributable to hawthorn. Hawthorn is moderately deep-rooted on clay soils. Growth rate is medium under good conditions. Suckering may be a problem.

Life expectancy is less than 50 years.

Both young and old trees tolerate heavy pruning.

See also under apple, pear and rowan.

# HORSE CHESTNUT  *Aesculus* species

1.  Maximum tree-to-damage distance recorded: 23 m. In 90 per cent of cases the tree was closer than 15 m.
2.  Normal maximum height in shrinkable clay urban areas: *Aesculus hippocastanum*, horse chestnut: 16–25 m but commonly near 20 m, *A. x carnea*, red horse chestnut: 12–16 m.
3.  Proportion of cases of damage occurring within certain bands of distance from the tree species on shrinkable clay soils:

| Cases of damage (%) | Distance from damage (m) |
|---------------------|--------------------------|
| 0 | Over 23 |
| 10 | 15–23 |
| 15 | 10–15 |
| 25 | 7.5–10 |
| 25 | 5–7.5 |
| 25 | 1.5–5 |

4.  Figure 3.10 is a graph showing the reduction in percentage of cases of damage recorded as the distance of trees from buildings increases (for shrinkable clay soils).

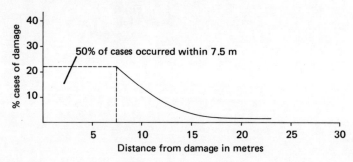

*Figure 3.10*

5a. Percentage of horse chestnut trees relative to the total for all trees reported to have caused damage: 2.9 per cent.
5b. Estimated percentage of horse chestnut trees used in street and garden planting relative to sample figures for all such tree plantings: 2.2 per cent.
6.  Percentage of cases of damage by horse chestnut trees involving shrinkable clay soils: over 98 per cent.
7.  Sample number: 63 cards; 323 additional identifications.

8.  Horse chestnut trees were involved in 11 per cent of all cases of tree damage to drains recorded.

*Note*: Little is known about the rooting habit in clay soils, but it is thought to be relatively shallow to moderately deep. Growth rate is fast under good conditions. Life expectancy is more than 100 years. Both young and old trees tolerate heavy pruning or crown reduction. Branches may be shed without warning. The fruits may be a nuisance.

# LIME   *Tilia* species

1. Maximum tree-to-damage distance recorded: 20 m. In 90 per cent of cases the tree was closer than 11 m.
2. Normal maximum height in shrinkable clay urban areas: *Tilia x europaea*, common lime: 21–24 m, *T. cordata*, small-leafed lime: 20 m, *T. euchlora*, Caucasian lime: 16–18 m.
3. Proportion of cases of damage occurring within certain bands of distance from the tree species on shrinkable clay soils:

| Cases of damage (%) | Distance from damage (m) |
|:---:|:---:|
| 0 | Over 20 |
| 10 | 11–20 |
| 15 | 8–11 |
| 25 | 6–8 |
| 25 | 4–6 |
| 25 | 1–4 |

4. Figure 3.11 is a graph showing the reduction in percentage of cases of damage recorded as the distance of trees from buildings increases (for shrinkable clay soils).

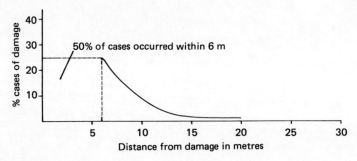

*Figure 3.11*

5.a Percentage of lime trees relative to the total for all trees reported to have caused damage: 8.2 per cent.
5b. Estimated percentage of lime trees used in street and garden planting relative to sample figures for all such tree plantings: 6.4 per cent.
6. Percentage of cases of damage by lime trees involving shrinkable clay soils: 100 per cent.
7. Sample number: 238 cards; 874 additional identifications.

42

8. Lime trees were involved in 1 per cent of all cases of damage to drains recorded.

*Notes*: Lime roots are moderately deep on clays soils. Growth rate is medium under good conditions. Life expectancy is over 100 years. Both young and old trees tolerate heavy pruning and crown reduction. Older trees frequently develop shoots around the base of the trunk. Trees are susceptible to aphid attack which produces sticky exudates of honeydew.

# OAK  *Quercus* species

1.  Maximum tree-to-damage distance recorded: 30 m. In 90 per cent of cases the tree was closer than 18 m.
2.  Normal maximum height in shrinkable clay urban areas: 16–23 m.
3.  Proportion of cases of damage occurring within certain bands of distance from the tree species on shrinkable clay soils:

    | *Cases of damage (%)* | *Distance from damage (m)* |
    |---|---|
    | 0 | Over 30 |
    | 10 | 18–30 |
    | 15 | 13–18 |
    | 25 | 9.5–13 |
    | 25 | 6–9.5 |
    | 25 | 1.3–6 |

4.  Figure 3.12 is a graph showing the reduction in percentage of cases of damage recorded as the distance of trees from buildings increases (for shrinkable clay soils).

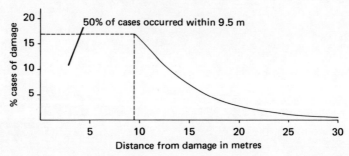

*Figure 3.12*

5a.  Percentage of oak trees relative to the total for all trees reported to have caused damage: 11.5 per cent.
5b.  Estimated percentage of oak trees used in street and garden planting relative to sample figures for all such tree plantings: 2.1 per cent.
6.  Percentage of cases of damage by oak trees involving shrinkable clay soils: 100 per cent.
7.  Sample number: 293 cards; 1253 additional identifications.
8.  Oak trees were involved in 3.5 per cent of all cases of tree damage to drains recorded.

*Notes*: Oak trees represented by the cards were almost all *Quercus robur* or *Q. petraea*. These two species are deep-rooted on clay soils.

The results of the survey indicate that oaks are potentially dangerous trees to plant near buildings on clay soils. In relation to their planting frequency they give the highest returns of reported damage.

Growth rate is medium in good conditions. Life expectancy is well over 100 years. Both young and old trees will tolerate heavy pruning and crown reduction. Branches may be shed without warning. Older trees may develop shoots around the base of the trunk. Oaks are susceptible to a wide variety of insect and fungal attack.

# PLANE  *Platanus* species

1. Maximum tree-to-damage distance recorded: 15 m. In 90 per cent of cases the tree was closer than 10 m.
2. Normal maximum height in shrinkable clay urban areas: *Platanus x hispanica:* 25–30 m.
3. Proportion of cases of damage occurring within certain bands of distance from the tree species on shrinkable clay soils:

| Cases of damage (%) | Distance from damage (m) |
|---|---|
| 0 | Over 15 |
| 10 | 10–15 |
| 15 | 7.5–10 |
| 25 | 5.5–7.5 |
| 25 | 4–5.5 |
| 25 | 1–4 |

4. Figure 3.13 is a graph showing the reduction in percentage of cases of damage recorded as the distance of trees from buildings increases (for shrinkable clay soils).

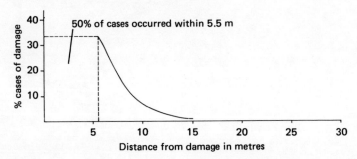

*Figure 3.13*

5a. Percentage of plane trees relative to the total for all trees reported to have caused damage: 11 per cent.
5b. Estimated percentage of plane trees used in street and garden planting relative to sample figures for all such tree plantings: 13.7 per cent.
6. Percentage of cases of damage by plane trees involving shrinkable clay soils: 100 per cent.
7. Sample number: 327 cards, 1140 additional identifications.
8. Plane trees were involved in 7.5 per cent of all cases of tree damage to drains recorded.

*Notes*: Planes are predominantly used as street trees. The distances at which a high proportion of reported damage occur are short (3 and 4 above), probably reflecting the average combined pavement/front garden measurements.

Planes are moderately deep-rooted on clay soils; they grow fast in good conditions. Life expectancy is over 100 years. Both young and old trees tolerate heavy pruning and crown reduction. Mature trees fruit freely.

# POPLAR  *Populus* species

1.  Maximum tree-to-damage distance recorded: 30 m. In 90 per cent of cases the tree was closer than 20 m.
2.  Normal maximum height in shrinkable clay urban areas: *Populus nigra 'Italica'*, Lombardy poplar: 25 m, *P. x euramericana 'Serotina'*, black Italian poplar: 28 m.
3.  Proportion of cases of damage occurring within certain bands of distance from the tree species on shrinkable clay soils:

| Cases of damage (%) | Distance from damage (m) |
|:---:|:---:|
| 0 | Over 30 |
| 10 | 20–30 |
| 15 | 15–20 |
| 25 | 11–15 |
| 25 | 6.5–11 |
| 25 | 1–6.5 |

4.  Figure 3.14 is a graph showing the reduction in percentage of cases of damage recorded as the distance of trees from buildings increases (for shrinkable clay soils).

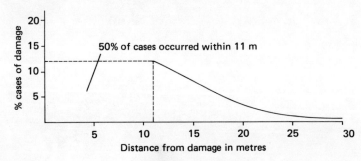

*Figure 3.14*

5a. Percentage of poplar trees relative to the total for all trees reported to have caused damage: 8.7 per cent.
5b. Estimated percentage of poplar trees used in street and garden planting relative to sample figures for all such tree plantings: 3 per cent.
6.  Percentage of cases of damage by poplar trees involving shrinkable clay soils: 99.5 per cent.
7.  Sample number: 191 cards; 974 additional identifications.

8. Poplar trees were involved in 24 per cent of all cases of tree
   damage to drains recorded.

*Notes*: Poplar and willow trees cannot be distinguished from each
other on root structure alone. The card sample number of 191
represents cases definitely attributable to poplar; 16 additional cases
were not definitely ascribed to either poplar or willow. Combined
figures for poplar and willow in the additional identifications have
been divided in the same ratio as for the card samples, and give a
reasonable guide to relative occurrence.

Poplar roots are deep in clay soils.

In relation to numbers planted, poplars came second to oaks in
this survey in the frequency with which they were associated with
damage to buildings.

Poplars grow fast in good conditions and have a life expectancy
of between 50 and 100 years. They may sucker, particularly from
damaged roots. Branches may be shed without warning. Both young
and old trees tolerate heavy pruning and crown reduction. Mature
female trees may produce hairy seeds which in quantity look like
cotton wool.

# ROWAN, SERVICE TREE, WHITE BEAM  *Sorbus* species

1. Maximum tree-to-damage distance recorded: 11 m. In 90 per cent of cases the tree was closer than 9.5 m.
2. Normal maximum height in shrinkable clay urban areas: *Sorbus aucuparia*, rowan: 11–12 m, other species of *Sorbus*: 8–12 m.
3. Proportion of cases of damage occurring within certain bands of distance from the tree species on shrinkable clay soils:

| Cases of damage (%) | Distance from damage (m) |
|---|---|
| 0 | Over 11 |
| 10 | 9.5–11 |
| 15 | 7–9.5 |
| 25 | 5–7 |
| 25 | 4–5 |
| 25 | 2.1–4 |

4. Figure 3.15 is a graph showing the reduction in percentage of cases of damage recorded as the distance of trees from buildings increases (for shrinkable clay soils).

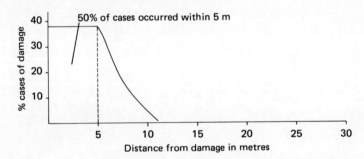

*Figure 3.15*

5a. Percentage of *Sorbus* trees relative to the total for all trees reported to have caused damage: 2.3 per cent.
5b. Estimated percentage of *Sorbus* trees used in street and garden planting relative to sample figures for all such tree plantings: 9.4 per cent.
6. Percentage of cases of damage by *Sorbus* trees involving shrinkable clay soils: 96 per cent.
7. Sample number: 32 cards; 271 additional identifications.

8. *Sorbus* trees were involved in less than 1 per cent of all cases of damage to drains recorded.

*Notes*: *Sorbus* species cannot be distinguished from each other on root structure alone. *Sorbus* roots can also be confused with those of apple, pear and hawthorn among trees. *Sorbus* may be grafted onto hawthorn stock. Growth rate is medium in good conditions. Life expectancy is between 50 and 100 years. Both young and old trees tolerate heavy pruning and crown reduction. Birds may be attracted by red- and orange-fruited trees.

# SYCAMORE, MAPLES   *Acer* species

1.  Maximum tree-to-damage distance recorded: 20 m. In 90 per cent of cases the tree was closer than 12 m.
2.  Normal maximum height in shrinkable clay urban areas: *Acer pseudoplatanus*, sycamore: 20–24 m, *A. platanoides*, Norway maple: 17–21 m, *A. negundo*, ash-leafed maple or box elder: 10–13 m.
3.  Proportion of cases of damage occurring within certain bands of distance from the tree species on shrinkable clay soils:

| Cases of damage (%) | Distance from damage (m) |
|:---:|:---:|
| 0 | Over 20 |
| 10 | 12–20 |
| 15 | 9–12 |
| 25 | 6–9 |
| 25 | 4–6 |
| 25 | 1–4 |

4.  Figure 3.16 is a graph showing the reduction in percentage of cases of damage recorded as the distance of trees from buildings increases (for shrinkable clay soils).

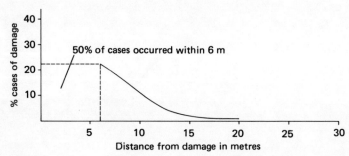

*Figure 3.16*

5a. Percentage of *Acer* trees relative to the total for all trees reported to have caused damage: 8.3 per cent.
5b. Estimated percentage of *Acer* trees used in street and garden planting relative to sample figures for all such tree planings: 13.9 per cent.
6.  Percentage of cases of damage of *Acer* trees involving shrinkable clay soils: 99 per cent.
7.  Sample number: 135 cards; 963 additional identifications

8.  *Acer* trees were involved in 9.6 per cent of all cases of tree damage to drains recorded.

*Notes*: *Acer* species cannot be distinguished from each other on root structure alone. The card entries indicated that 78 per cent of enquiries related to sycamore. Only 2 per cent related to dwarf species or varieties.

Large *Acer* species are deep-rooting on clay soils. Dwarf species are slow growing, but larger species grow fast in good conditions. Life expectancy can exceed 100 years. Some species fruit freely and the resultant seedlings may cause problems. Aphid attack may result in honeydew formation. Young and older trees of the larger species tolerate heavy pruning and crown reduction.

# WILLOW  *Salix* species

1. Maximum tree-to-damage distance recorded: 40 m. In 90 per cent of cases the tree was closer than 18 m.
2. Normal maximum height in shrinkable clay urban areas: the majority are below 15 m but some trees can attain 20–25 m.
3. Proportion of cases of damage occurring within certain bands of distance from the tree species on shrinkable clay soils:

| Cases of damage (%) | Distance from damage (m) |
| --- | --- |
| 0 | Over 40 |
| 10 | 18–40 |
| 15 | 11–18 |
| 25 | 7–11 |
| 25 | 4.5–7 |
| 25 | 1–4.5 |

4. Figure 3.17 is a graph showing the reduction in percentage of cases of damage recorded as the distance of trees from buildings increases (for shrinkable clay soils).

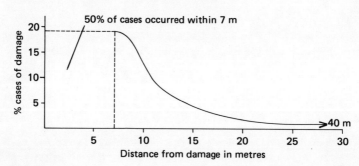

*Figure 3.17*

5a. Percentage of willow trees relative to the total for all trees reported to have caused damage: 5.7 per cent.
5b. Estimated percentage of willow trees used in street and garden planting relative to sample figures for all such tree plantings: 4.5 per cent.
6. Percentage of cases of damage by willow trees involving shrinkable clay soils: 100 per cent.
7. Sample number: 124 cards; 633 additional identifications.
8. Willow trees were involved in 18.5 per cent of all cases of tree damage to drains recorded.

*Notes*: Willow and poplar trees cannot be distinguished from each other on root structure alone. The card sample number of 124 represents cases definitely attributable to willow. See also notes for Poplar.

Willow roots are moderately deep in clay soils.

Some examples of willow have the largest root spread recorded in the survey. Willows are fast growing in good conditions; trees have a life expectancy of between 50 and 100 years. Both young and old trees tolerate heavy pruning and crown thinning. They may sucker freely. Branches may be shed without warning.

# Notes for use in conjunction with the brief entries for trees

Trees could appear in this section either if the types concerned genuinely cause little damage to buildings under the normal range of planting conditions, or if they are so rarely planted that the frequency with which damage reports arose was similarly low.

Trees in the second category might give rise to subsidence problems, but with such sparse information no sound conclusions could be drawn.

Because there are so few records it was not possible to give extended entries for these trees, and only four main items were included:

1. Maximum tree-to-damage distance recorded. These figures must serve only as a rough guide.
2. Normal maximum height in shrinkable clay urban areas. This information is more reliable; it is based on wider observations.
3. Percentage of cases of damage by the particular tree involving shrinkable clay soils. The value of this information is limited by the very small sample number.
4. Sample number. The number of samples investigated will give a guide to the reliance that can be placed on data in items 1 and 3 of the brief entries. They do not include returns for diseased or blown-down trees.

The exclusion of certain sorts of tree from these entries does not imply that they are safe close to buildings on clay soils. Some uncommon trees do not appear in the survey records. A few, listed below, have been rarely associated with damage:

Sweet Chestnut (*Castanea sativa*) 6;
Mulberry (*Morus* species) 4;
Indian bean tree (*Catalpa* species) 3;
Tamarisk (*Tamarix* species) 1;
Tulip tree (*Liriodendron tulipifera*) 1

## ALDER  *Alnus* species

1. Maximum tree-to-damage distance recorded: 4 m.
2. Normal maximum height in shrinkable clay urban areas: *Alnus glutinosa*: 15 m, *A. cordata*: 17–20 m.
3. Percentage of cases of damage by alder involving shrinkable clay soils: 100 per cent.

57

4. Sample number: 1 card, 5 additional identifications.

*Notes*: Rarely planted, except on reclamation sites. Growth rate is medium in good conditions. Life expectancy is between 50 and 100 years. Both young and old trees tolerate heavy pruning or crown reduction. Alders may sucker, and are susceptible to aphid attack.

## ELDER   *Sambucus nigra*

1. Maximum tree-to-damage distance recorded: 8 m.
2. Normal maximum height in shrinkable clay urban areas: 6–7 m.
3. Percentage of cases of damage by elder involving shrinkable clay soils: 100 per cent.
4. Sample number: 13 cards; 219 additional identifications.

*Notes*: Fast growing, small tree, with a life expectancy of under 50 years. Both young and old trees tolerate heavy pruning.

## FIG   *Ficus carica*

1. Maximum tree-to-damage distance recorded: 5 m.
2. Normal maximum height in shrinkable clay soil urban areas: 6 m.
3. Percentage of cases of damage by fig involving shrinkable clay soils: 100 per cent.
4. Sample number: 3 cards; 9 additional identifications.

*Notes*: Usually restricted by pruning and limitation of root run to induce fruiting. Not commonly planted; has life expectancy of 50–60 years.

## HAZEL   *Corylus avellana*

1. Maximum tree-to-damage distance recorded: 3 m.
2. Normal maximum height in shrinkable clay urban areas: 10 m.
3. Percentage of cases of damage by hazel involving shrinkable clay soils: 100 per cent.
4. Sample number: 1 card; 11 additional identifications.

*Notes*: Rarely planted in urban areas, except as the 'contorted' and purple forms. Growth rate is medium in good conditions. Life expectancy is under 50 years unless coppiced. Both young and old trees tolerate heavy pruning.

## HOLLY   *Ilex aquifolium*

1. Maximum tree-to-damage distance recorded: 3 m.

2. Normal maximum height in shrinkable clay urban areas: 12–14 m.
3. Percentage of cases of damage by holly involving shrinkable clay soils: 100 per cent.
4. Sample number: 2 cards; 7 additional identifications.

*Notes*: Slow-growing; life expectancy between 50 and 100 years. Both young and old trees tolerate heavy pruning.

## HORNBEAM  *Carpinus betulus*

1. Maximum tree-to-damage distance recorded: 17 m.
2. Normal maximum height in shrinkable clay urban areas: typical variety: 17–18 m, var. *fastigiata*: 12 m.
3. Percentage of cases of damage by hornbeam involving shrinkable clay soils: 100 per cent.
4. Sample number: 8 cards, 61 additional identifications.

*Notes*: The fastigiate variety is increasing in popularity for street planting. Growth rate is medium in good conditions, life expectancy is more than 100 years.

## LABURNUM  *Laburnum* species

1. Maximum tree-to-damage distance recorded: 7 m.
2. Normal maximum height in shrinkable clay urban areas: 7–9 m.
3. Percentage of cases of damage by laburnum involving shrinkable clay soils: 84 per cent.
4. Sample number: 7 cards; see under false acacia for additional identifications.

*Notes*: Laburnum seeds are poisonous. The tree is fast growing in good conditions; life expectancy is less than 50 years. Young trees will tolerate heavy, but old trees only light, pruning.

## LILAC  *Syringa vulgaris*

1. Maximum tree-to-damage distance recorded: 4 m.
2. Normal maximum height in shrinkable clay urban areas: 7–8 m.
3. Percentage of cases of damage by lilac involving shrinkable clay soils: 89 per cent.
4. Sample number: 9 cards. Additional identifications are accounted for in the shrub entries under Oleaceae.

*Notes*: Suckers readily; growth rate is fast in good conditions. Life expectancy is less than 50 years. Young trees tolerate heavy, and older trees light, pruning.

## LOCUST TREE   *Gleditsia triacanthos*

1. Maximum tree-to-damage distance recorded: 15 m.
2. Normal maximum height in shrinkable clay urban areas: 13–16 m.
3. Percentage of cases of damage by *Gleditsia* involving shrinkable clay soils: 100 per cent.
4. Sample number: 1 card.

*Notes*: This single example was a 12 m tall tree. The species is rarely planted. It is tender, only growing well in the South and West. It is slow growing, and will live for between 50 and 100 years. Young trees tolerate heavy, and old trees only light, pruning.

## MAGNOLIA   *Magnolia* species

1. Maximum tree-to-damage distance recorded: 5 m.
2. Normal maximum height in shrinkable clay urban areas: *Magnolia x soulangeana*: 5–7 m.
3. Percentage of cases of damage by *Magnolia* involving shrinkable clay soils: 100 per cent.
4. Sample number: 2 cards; 12 additional identifications.

*Notes*: *Magnolia grandiflora* is commonly planted as a wall shrub. The very low return of instances of damage is notable.

## PAGODA TREE   *Sophora japonica*

1. Maximum tree-to-damage distance recorded: 3 m.
2. Normal maximum height in shrinkable clay urban areas: 14–16 m.
3. Percentage of cases of damage by *Sophora* involving shrinkable clay soils: 100 per cent.
4. Sample number: 1 card.

*Notes*: This single example was a 3 m-tall specimen. The species is rarely planted. Growth rate is medium in suitable conditions. Life expectancy is normally between 50 and 100 years. Young trees tolerate heavy, and old trees only light, pruning.

# TREE OF HEAVEN   *Ailanthus* species

1. Maximum tree-to-damage distance recorded: 3 m.
2. Normal maximum height in shrinkable clay urban areas: 18–22 m.
3. Percentage of cases of damage by *Ailanthus* involving shrinkable clay soils: 100 per cent.
4. Sample number: 2 cards; 39 additional identifications.

*Notes*: Prone to produce sucker shoots which will develop into trees if allowed. Fast growing, the tree has a life expectancy of 50 to 100 years. Both young and old trees tolerate heavy pruning.

# WALNUT   *Juglans regia*

1. Maximum tree-to-damage distance recorded: 8 m.
2. Normal maximum height in shrinkable clay urban areas: 12–15 m.
3. Percentage of cases of damage by walnut involving shrinkable clay soils: 100 per cent.
4. Sample number: 3 cards; 15 additional identifications.

*Notes*: No cards were returned for the black walnut, *Juglans nigra*. This species is rarely grown, except in urban parks, and has a normal maximum height in shrinkable clay urban areas of 18–23 m. Growth rate is medium in good conditions. Life expectancy is over 100 years. Branches may be shed without warning. Young trees tolerate heavy, and old trees light, pruning, but only when in full leaf.

# CONIFERS

The proportion of conifers in relation to all trees reported to have damaged buildings is low.

The planting frequency figures available for conifers included large numbers of dwarf ornamentals. Because of this it was not possible to make strict comparisons with the planting frequency data for broad-leaved trees. Street planting of conifers is very uncommon. Consequently it was thought best to treat all the data on conifers separately. In the longer entry for Cypress, however, the planting frequency was estimated with reference to the data for broad-leaved trees, as was the percentage of involvement in drain damage.

The ultimate height of many conifers grown in Britain is not known, most are still growing. The mature height figures for conifers in clay soils are, therefore, only estimates.

Most of the larger conifers are medium to fast growing and have a life expectancy of over 100 years. The majority will tolerate only light pruning when young or mature, but yews respond well to pruning or crown reduction. Suckering is rare, except in yew, when twigs may arise around the base of the trunk.

Figures for types of conifers other than Cypress mostly relate to

Table 3.1 Card returns showing subsidence damage attributable to conifers.

| | No. of cards for damage on clay soil | Urban mature height (m) | Maximum distance from damage recorded (m) | No. of other cards returned (mostly from trees blown down) | Rooting habit |
|---|---|---|---|---|---|
| Cupressus, Cypresses* (*Cupressaceae*) | 31+376[†] | 12–25 | 20 | 12 | Moderately deep, dense |
| Firs (*Abies*) | 1 | 15–20 | 2 | 2 | Deep |
| Monkey puzzle (*Araucaria*) | 2 | 15–18+ | 3 | — | ? |
| Pines (*Pinus*) | 5+43[†] | 20–29 | 8 | 36 | *P. sylvestris* shallow *P. nigra* deep |
| Redwoods (*Sequoia*) | 1+1[†] | 17–23 | 1 | — | Deep |
| Yew (*Taxus*) | 1+36[†] | 8–12 | 5 | — | ? |

* These data are given in fuller form on pp. 64–65.
† additional identifications, and 39 additional unspecified conifers.

trees which had been blown down. Many of these were not in urban areas. They were: cedars (*Cedrus*), 12; *Cryptomeria*, 1; Douglas fir (*Pseudotsuga*), 8; hemlocks (*Tsuga*), 2; incense cedar (*Calocedrus*), 1; junipers (*Juniperus*), 1; larch (*Larix*), 7; spruces (*Picea*), 8; western red cedar (*Thuja*), 1. Maiden-hair tree (*Ginkgo*), 1.

# CYPRESSES, CUPRESSUS,
*Cupressus* and *Chamaecyparis* species

1. Maximum tree-to-damage distance recorded: 20 m. In 90 per cent of cases the tree was closer than 5 m.
2. Normal maximum height in shrinkable clay urban areas: *Chamaecyparis lawsoniana*, Lawson's cypress: 15–22 m, *Cupressus macrocarpa*, Monterey cypress: 18–25 m.
3. Proportion of cases of damage occurring within certain bands of distance from the tree species on shrinkable clay soils:

| Cases of damage (%) | Distance from damage (m) |
|:---:|:---:|
| 0 | Over 20 |
| 10 | 5–20 |
| 15 | 3.5–5 |
| 25 | 2.5–3.5 |
| 25 | 1.5–2.5 |
| 25 | 1–1.5 |

4. Figure 3.18 is a graph showing the reduction in percentage of cases of damage recorded as the distance of trees from buildings increases (for shrinkable clay soils).

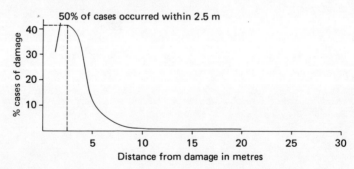

*Figure 3.18*

5a. Percentage of cypress trees relative to the total for all trees reported to have caused damage: 3 per cent.
5b. Estimated percentage of cypress trees used in street and garden planting relative to sample figures for all such tree plantings: about 10 per cent.
6. Percentage of cases of damage by cypress trees involving shrinkable clay soils: 100 per cent.

7.  Sample number: 31 cards; 376 additional identifications.
8.  Cypress trees were involved in about 2.5 per cent of all tree damage to drains recorded.

*Notes*: Members of the family Cupressaceae cannot be distinguished from each other by root structure alone. The roots of both *Chamaecyparis lawsoniana* and *Cupressus macrocarpa* are moderately deep on clay soils. See also introduction to section on conifers, p. 62.

# SHRUBS

Table 3.2 *Shrub root identifications – combined data from survey cards and 1979–86 records*

| | |
|---|---:|
| *Ampelopsis* – see Vitaceae | |
| Berberidaceae (*Berberis, Mahonia*) | 31 |
| *Buddleja* | 1 |
| *Camellia* | 1 |
| Caprifoliaceae (*Lonicera, Symphoricarpos, Viburnum, Weigela*) | 76 |
| *Chaenomeles* (Japonica) – see also Pomoideae under Tree entries, p. 25 | 5 |
| *Clematis* | 2 |
| *Cotinus* (Smoke Bush) – see *Rhus* | |
| *Cotoneaster* – see also Pomoideae | 3 |
| *Cydonia* (Quince) – see also Pomoideae | 1 |
| *Euonymus* (Spindleberry) | 3 |
| *Fatsia* – see *Hedera* | 3 |
| *Forsythia* – see Oleaceae | |
| *Fuchsia* | 6 |
| *Hebe* | 1 |
| *Hedera* (Ivy); probably includes some *Fatsia* | 27 |
| *Hydrangea* | 27 |
| *Jasminum* (Jasmine) – see Oleaceae | |
| *Kerria* – see Rosoideae | |
| *Ligustrum* (Privet) – see Oleaceae | |
| *Lonicera* (Honeysuckle) – see Caprifoliaceae | |
| *Mahonia* – see Berberidaceae | |
| Oleaceae (*Forsythia, Jasminum, Ligustrum, Syringa*) | 354 |
| *Parthenocissus* (Virginia Creeper) – see Vitaceae | |
| *Philadelphus* (Mock Orange) | 13 |
| *Pittosporum* | 1 |
| Pomoideae – see tree entry for Apple, pp. 24, 25 | |
| *Prunus* – see tree entry for Cherries, p. 32 | |
| *Polygonum* (Russian Vine) | 1 |
| *Potentilla* – see Rosoideae | |
| *Pyracantha* (Firethorn) – see also Pomoideae | 9 |
| *Rhododendron* | 1 |
| *Rhus* (Sumach) and *Cotinus* | 2 |
| *Ribes* (Currant) | 4 |
| *Rosa* (Rose) – see Rosoideae | |
| Rosoideae (*Kerria, Potentilla, Rosa, Rubus*) | 367 |
| *Rubus* (Bramble) – see Rosoideae | |
| *Sambucus* (Elder) – see brief tree entries, p. 58 | |
| *Symphoricarpos* (snowberry) – see Caprifoliaeceae | |
| *Syringa* (Lilac) – see Oleaceae and brief tree entries, p. 59 | |
| *Viburnum* (Guelder Rose) – see Caprifoliaceae | |
| Vitaceae (*Ampelopsis, Parthenocissus, Vitis*) | 69 |
| *Vitis* (vine) – see Vitaceae | |
| *Weigela* – see Caprifoliaceae | |
| *Wisteria* | 1 |

It is very difficult to apportion 'blame' when roots of a large tree and those from shrubs are found together in an inspection hole in clay soil near damaged buildings. Normally the tree might be expected to have been the major contributor to the damage although the additional drying effect of shrub roots could have contributed. Small shrubs, and in particular roses, are very unlikely on their own to be involved in damage. Shrubs are often shallow-rooted, though roots of climbers may run alongside a wall for considerable distances. Groups of large shrubs can dry soils considerably.

The records on p. 66 are included here because those concerned with the particular investigations thought that the shrubs were implicated in damage to some extent. There are more extensive records where shrub roots were identified, most often together with tree roots. These shrubs were judged by the site investigators to be of little significance, and are consequently omitted from this account.

Shrubs of different types are often planted together. Frequently several members of a closely related group can not be separated on root identification alone, and data relating to them are put together in the list (Table 3.2) since planting details were not available.

# Selected Bibliography

Aldous, T (Ed.), (1979) *Trees and Buildings. Complement or Conflict?*, RIBA and Tree Council Publication.

Biddle, P G (1979) 'Tree root damage to buildings – an arboriculturist's experience', *Arbor. J.* **3**, 397–412.

Biddle, P G (1983) 'Patterns of soil drying and moisture deficit in the vicinity of trees on clay soils', *Geotechnique*, **33**(2), 107–126.

Binns, W O (1980) 'Trees and water', *Forestry Commission Arboricultural Leaflet*, No. 6, HMSO, London.

British Standards Institution (1980), '*Code of Practice for Trees in Relation to Construction*', London.

Building Research Establishment (1965, 1972, 1976) 'Soils and foundations', 1–3, *Digests 63, 64, 67*, BRE.

Building Research Establishment (1980) 'Low-rise buildings on shrinkable clay soils', 1–3, *Digests 240, 241, 242*, BRE.

Building Research Establishment (1965) 'The influence of trees on house foundations in clay soils', *Digest 298*, BRE.

Cheney, J E and Burford, D (1974) 'Damaging uplift to a three-storey office block constructed on a clay soil following the removal of trees', *Proc. Conf. on Settlement of Structures*, Cambridge, pp. 337–43.

Cutler, D F (1974) 'Tree root Damage to buildings', *J. Inst. Wood Science*, **6**(6), 9–12.

Cutler, D F (1978) 'Survey and identification of tree Roots', *Arbor. J.* **3** 243–246.

Cutler, D F, Rudall, P J, Gasson, P E and Gale, R M O (1987) *Root identification manual of Trees and Shrubs*, Chapman & Hall.

Driscoll, R M C (1983) 'The influence of vegetation on the swelling and shrinking of clay in Britain', *Geotechnique* **33**(2), 93–105.

Edlin, H L (1970) 'Know your conifers', *Forestry Commission Booklet*, No. 15, HMSO, London.

Edlin, H L and Darter C (1975) 'Know your broadleaves', *Forestry Commission Booklet*, No. 20, HMSO, London.

Holtz, W G (1959) 'Expansive clay – properties and problems', *Colorado School of Mines Quarterly*, **54**, No. 4.

Mitchell, A (1974) *A Field Guide to the Trees of Britain and Northern Europe*, Collins, London.

NHBC (1974) 'Root damages by Trees – Siting of Dwellings and Special Precautions' *Practice Note 3* London.

NHBC (1985, 1986) 'Building near trees', *Practice Note 3 and Supplement*, London.

Reece, R A (1979) 'Trees and insurance', *Arbor. J.* **3**, 492–499.

Reynolds, E R C *1979) A Report on Tree Roots and Built Development*, DOE.

Samuels, S G (1974) and Cheney, J E 'Long-term heave of a building on clay due to tree removal', *Proc. Conf. on Settlement of Structures*, Cambridge, pp 212–220.

Tomlinson, M J, Driscoll, R and Burland, J B, (1978) 'Foundations for low-rise buildings', *The Structural Engineer*, **56A**, 161–173.

# Index

*Index*

70